Breathe Life Into Your Day!

*Inspirational Quotes & Reflections to **Refresh**, **Renew**, and **Re-calibrate** Your Mind, Body, and Soul for Wellness*

Dr. Lisa Cook

Dr. Lisa Cook, LCPC, LPCC, LPC, CPC. Breathe Life Into Your Day ~ Inspirational Quotes & Reflections to Refresh, Renew, and Re-calibrate to Your Mind, Body, and Soul for Wellness. Copyright © 2025

All Rights Reserved. Printed in the United States of America.

All rights reserved. No portion of this book may be reproduced in any form without the publisher's prior permission, except as permitted by U.S. copyright law. For permissions, contact:

drlcook@lifeimpactcirclesofwellness.com

Life Impact Circles of Wellness

Editing: Jarvis C.

Book Cover: Noman Abid

ISBN: 978-1-7345361-6-4

Acknowledgements

Special thanks to God for providing me with the gift of inspiration to uplift others and the skills to encourage individuals through my words spoken audibly or in written form.

When you understand your purpose, the outflow of your purpose exudes through your life. I walk in my purpose, and it is to create Life Impact!

To each reader or listener, I stand at the pond of water and I throw in my pebbles. When those pebbles hit the water, I see the ripples spreading outward. I hope that my pebbles in the water will ripple into your life to create a profound impact.

Breathe life into your day!

I found the power of breath!
A real acknowledged breath!
A **Breath** that allows you to be!
A **Breath** that ignites change!
A **Breath** that propels calm to the mind, body and spirit!
A **Breath** that expels the weight of the moment to God!

A **Breath** that allows you to live!

The act of breathing, divinely supplied in God's creation, provides life sustainability, offers calm to the nervous system and can empower us to create a meaningful existence for ourselves by *Breathing Life Into Your Day*.

Table of Contents

Acknowledgements	3
Power of Positivity	6
By Faith, Show Up for Your Life	28
Empowering You: Body, Mind and Spirit	57
Embracing Love & Compassion for Yourself	81
Purposeful Living	104
Transcending Higher	125
References	150

Power of Positivity

So, it begins...with you. Positivity is a belief system; it is a disposition; it is a perception, and it is a choice. Harness its power to transform your life!

Our positive impact commences from our positive perspective and internal conversations within ourselves. When we approach life with this viewpoint, combined with mental reframing and faith, it acts as **kryptonite** to all negative forces that come against us.

Time to Reflect...

What thoughts, attitudes or actions do you need to channel your power at this moment? What areas of your mind need to be rewired to create a positive perspective?

Never give up on your **dreams**, even if they seem far-fetched to someone else, it does not matter...because your dreams belong to **YOU**! You hold the perseverance and prerogative to move your dreams into your reality!

Time to Reflect...
If you have allowed your dreams to drift away, what efforts are necessary to reclaim your dreams to move them towards living your purpose?

As you commence your day, remember that every issue is within the realm of your capacity to find a solution. Tap into your ingenuity, your resources and your historical blueprint that solidifies that you are indeed a **"Solution Maker."**

Time to Reflect...

Since you are a "Solution Maker", how will this truth allow you to navigate this day? Does the possibility of creating a solution foster tension or physical stress? If so, take the breaths needed to bring calm to your body and to support reframing your perception. Draw on the empirical evidence of your historical resilience and creativity and then move forward with persistence.

Never let the **"Nos"** in life keep you from your destination!

Time to Reflect...

What is your plan to eliminate the "No's" that are generated in your internal thoughts, and how can you redirect the "No's" presented to you from external sources?

It takes **absolutely nothing** for us to demonstrate **kindness** to a person that may or may not reciprocate kindness to us. The law of reciprocity tells us that our acts of kindness will come back to us...when we need it the most!

Time to Reflect...

Are you allowing the vessel of kindness inside of you the permission to show up, or could any feelings of fear, anger, insecurity, or possible judgement override your kindness?

If no one has shared this fact with you, "You are **appreciated for the uniqueness of your being!"**

Time to Reflect...

Since there is absolutely no one like you on this planet, why are you letting the opinions of others stifle the exceptionalism of YOU?

Never diminish your voice...**SPEAK**, because you have something of **value** to say! ~

Time to Reflect...

What if you spent your lifetime without sharing the profound wisdom that is in you? The world would be less equipped because we never heard your voice...SPEAK!

Sometimes, you can surprise others with your greatness but never let it be a surprise to yourself!! **Recognize YOU!**

Time to Reflect...

How are you measuring your greatness? Look in the mirror and accept the person looking at you...You are great! No judgment! No internal critic! Turn on your internal cheerleader...You Stand Alone as YOU!

Let us be thankful for **our ability** to shift our perspective from how we are perceived by others to how we perceive ourselves and the world. Our perception is **EVERYTHING!**

Time to Reflect...

What is the one area that you can start to shift your perspective into a favorable and positive space? As you navigate the various spaces of your life, challenge your perception if you notice that it creates internal suffering. Take the time to understand what drives your perception and pursue one thing that validates your needs, the facts, and your heart.

Give space and time for your **rest, renewal, reflection, and relationships** to cultivate the inclusivity of **peace and laughter**. These are **irreplaceable** moments of life!

Time to Reflect...

How can I replace my chaos with peace and my angst with laughter? What will be my next steps towards these irreplaceable life moments?

Let us strive to **push past** the difficult moments or the barriers to keep our internal seeds of growth **alive and vibrant**! Let your roses live!!

Time to Reflect...

Are you caught up with the thorns of life? Remember that you still have roses available to you, despite past experiences. Your roses could be right in front of you! What can you do to find your roses?

One of the ways that we can maximize our energy could be...to do our best to **GET REST!** Deliver us from the culture that celebrates exhaustion (physical, emotional, psychological, etc.)! Our obligation is to be accountable to ourselves, our mission, and our purpose each day, and **getting the proper rest** is vital to one's ability to be **present, balanced, and productive** each day!

Time to Reflect...

Energy equates to power. How much of your power is focused towards resting your mind, calming your thoughts, and soothing your body from anxiousness? Showing up and being present means you will experience more of life!

Embrace who you are...your gifts, your strengths and every facet that makes you uniquely YOU! **You were built for whatever situation that you are facing right NOW!**

Time to Reflect...

What would your day or life look like if you decided to embrace yourself versus embracing your insecurities?

Can you embrace your capabilities rather than dwelling on your failures or mistakes? What belief could you shift?

We all carry so much on our plates, but remember that **self-awareness, self-care, and the power of positivity are valuable assets** for us to manage through life's unpredictability!

Time to Reflect...

Challenge yourself to think of 5 positive things each day...watch your assessment of life transform!

As you start this day, seek to be free and allow the true essence of yourself to **SHINE, GLOW and FLOW! Freedom** looks good on **YOU!**

Time to Reflect...

What would it be like if you totally stopped caring about what others think about you? Celebrate YOUR FREEDOM from people's opinions and CELEBRATE your ability to win!

Every day that we wake up is an opportunity to **live life!** Tell someone that you love them! Go somewhere you have always wanted to go! **Dance, sing, run, shout...just do something that is good for you!** Life is a precious gift, and we do not get any do-overs! Make every second count!

Time to Reflect...

What is the first thing you will do to live life on this day?

Create a 30-day Life Plan to find the moments that can bring you joy.

Sometimes, it is the intangibles that count the most. Helen Keller was blind, **but she was able to see!** What are the intangibles that you can see today that speak to your heart?

Time to Reflect...

Are you walking through life blind and missing out on the beauty that life brings? Take a moment to look around.

What do you see?

What makes your heart smile?

What fosters peace or creativity?

What can you discover about YOU, with your new ability to see the intangibles?

You are **NOT** the person that your TRAUMA experiences tell you that you are!

Time to Reflect...

Trauma terrorizes. Trauma immobilizes. Trauma lies to you. Take a minute to bring awareness to the falsehoods that trauma has breed into your life. There is freedom on the other side of this discovery!

Seek, if you can, to find the truths to the falsehoods that counter those harmful narratives to build your mind towards helpful, positive and productive thinking.

Even a **fragile voice is powerful**...it is about the message being conveyed! Each of us has something important and valuable to say...so let it flow!

Time to Reflect...
What is the message that you have wrapped up in your heart? Write it down...share it! What comes from the heart reaches the heart!

It is up to you...but consuming your time to be happy versus being sad seems like **a winning investment** in yourself.

You can impact your entire environment...simply by choosing happiness.

Time to Reflect...

Miraculously, we can train our bodies and minds to be a conveyor of happiness...work at this! When you contemplate how much you are expending to be sad, can you picture yourself capturing happiness and your voice at the same time? Journal about your next steps to live out this quote.

Recognize your ability to set a **daily intention** with yourself and your relationships by **sending positive vibes and positive affirmations.** Declare to yourself internally and audibly, "I will create and cultivate my climate in the positive realm."

Time to Reflect...

Creating the desired energy in your life begins with self-belief, the language you nurture, and the effort you invest. Explore ways to articulate five positive affirmations about yourself and your relationships each day.

By Faith, Show Up for Your Life

Faith shows the reality of what we hope for; it is the evidence of things we cannot see. Hebrews 11:1

We all have faith...it is a matter of what and whom you choose to have faith in.

You are not alone in your journey of life! There is a **collective symphony rooting** for you!

Time to Reflect...

The Bible tells us that "we are surrounded by a great cloud of witnesses" this enables us to trust that we have someone looking over us to keep going in life.

What area of your life have you felt alone?

Who comes to mind that can be included in the "great cloud of witnesses" (Hebrews 12:1) that is rooting for your journey?

Just in case, you did not know…it is your **God given right to shine** in everything that you do! **You** are **amazingly brilliant** and possess a multitude of **talents,** and you possess **spiritual gifts**!

Time to Reflect...

When you rise every morning, look in the mirror and expect to see your shine! Tell yourself you were created in the image of God, so it is innate in you to shine through His glory! Walk in this TRUTH!

Fear can hinder your ability to take steps towards your destiny and living authentically, whereas **Faith** can enable you to move beyond the impossibilities to the probabilities to achieve what is possible in your life's journey.

Time to Reflect...

Consider the practice of listing out when you are afraid and when you have faith in situations. Evaluate your findings, can you determine the position that serves you? Will you choose immobilization or the possibilities of purpose for today?

"Lord Help" ...these two simple words have prevailing and profound results in one's life.

Time to Reflect...

In desperate moments of life, we tend to cry out to God for help. In Psalms 107, these two simple words are repeated at least six times, indicating that verbalizing, "Lord Help", there is certainty in producing prevailing and profound results. The potentiality of these two words can usher in the authority, the presence, and the providence of God in your life!

Food for Thought~

The significance of invoking "Lord Help" exemplifies the mercy and love that God extends to humanity.

Consider how frequently individuals make decisions based on their own judgment with the belief that these choices to be the best for their lives.

When such decisions lead to disappointing or destructive outcomes, pain, or challenging circumstances, they often create a form of distress.

When the impact of decisions is not necessarily caused by one's own actions, they may often result in trauma or adverse consequences.

Here's the reality…if you just cry out to God in sincerity, He is obligated to Himself to be faithful and to show up for you!

These two simple words usher a release of a divine reactionary response to momentary faith into your life as you believe in God and in your expectation of who He says He is!

If you have the need in your life, I encourage you by faith to call on Him! "Lord Help!"

I'm convinced that you are going to walk in your **capability** and **be okay**! You know why? Because everything that Satan and the powers of darkness use to try to capture you are **STILL** subjected to the **ultimate sovereignty of God**.

Time to Reflect...

Remember who you are…and if you do not know who you are, commence the reflective journey to discover the power you possess based on being YOU, since God loves you.

"And I am convinced that nothing can ever separate us from God's love. Neither death nor life, neither angels nor demons, neither our fears for today nor our worries for tomorrow ---not even the powers of hell can separate us from God's love." Romans 8:38

Spend at least 5 minutes each day reminding and reflecting about who you are and who God created you to be!

So, if God commits to it, then He builds the **CONTINUITY** in our lives to complete His Word to Himself and for us! It's up to us to align ourselves within the course of the **continuity of His promises**!

Time to Reflect...

"He always stands by his covenant — the commitment he made to a thousand generations."
Psalms 105:8 NLT

The Continuity of God's Promises lets us know that we will be OKAY!
You will be HEALED!
You will be HEALTHY!!
You will have ANSWERED PRAYERS!
You will WALK IN THE SPHERE of GOD'S GRACE!!
You will RECEIVE MERCIES EACH DAY!

Think about what God has done in your life, then chronicle the consistent **blessings** and **miracles** from your life! After noting the benefits, you have received from God, then you can grasp what a privilege you have to offer **God blessings!!** The word blessings mean to boast; to speak well of abundantly. Just think about how much you have to say!!

Time to Reflect...

Even when we don't feel like it, God must be spoken well of or boasted about just because He is God!! But when we ponder what He has done, what He is doing and what He will do. Marvel...because this is something that can yield excitement and joy!

Take this opportunity for a praise break right now!!

My hope is that you lean on God by **faith** and rest in His ability for your **rescues**.

Time to Reflect...

"For He will rescue you from every trap and protect you from deadly disease." Psalms 91:3

As a clinician, I understand that a portion of the work of therapy is often about the RESCUES! Rescue means to save (someone) from a dangerous or distressing situation (an actionable event).

When life presents pressure, it is our nervous system that reacts to the experience, then our mind, body and emotions influence our behaviours!

The autonomic nervous system within our body relays signals to the amygdala in the brain, which facilitates our emergency responses. Whether we move towards fight, freeze, flop, flight, or fawn in a situation, our conditioned wiring will show up based on our historical footprints.

The goal is learning the art of the rescue to bring a reset to your mind, body, heart, and spirit…

- *Whether it is through prayer, seeking God's presence and the Holy Spirit's comfort.*
- *Whether it is meditation to calm your thoughts and emotions, to what is really happening versus what your triggers are perceiving.*
- *Whether it is taking deep breaths or sleeping on a situation before you react, God has equipped us all with a RESCUE!*

Sometimes, He is performing a miraculous deliverance, and sometimes He is asking you and I to operate in faith to walk into our safety!

My hope today is that you lean towards Him and lean towards your strength for your RESCUE!

DEEP BREATH...because you have life! Now...**EXHALE** since God has your life in His hands!

Time to Reflect...

Just think...every living thing that has been created owes its life to God! But in humanity, God gives us an opportunity for a relationship with Him that is different from all creation. If you choose to seek Him, you will find that a relationship with Him is the most rewarding investment, intersection, intimacy, and involvement you can have to manifest exactly what your life needs! Life doesn't get easier with God, it gets BETTER, despite the rough times.

"Our lives are in His hand and He keeps our feet from stumbling...Psalms 66:9" NLT

There is a **REWARD** for the **RETURN!** When God brings us back from exile (separation or isolation) by **CHOICE** or by **FORCE…THE REUNIFICATION** with Him is **GLORY!**

Time to Reflect…

A REWARD For Our RETURN! When God brings us back from exile (any place where you experienced loneliness, sadness, grief, and separation from His presence or an arrogant attitude possessing no need of Him) by choice or by force…the reunification with Him is GLORY!! Whenever we are afforded an opportunity to reunite in our relationship with God, it's a place of renewal, rejuvenation, refreshment and reflection of His kindness and grace to our lives!

Do you want to reunite with Him? Take time in your daily routine to connect with God.
"When the Lord brought back his exiles to Jerusalem, it was like a dream! We were filled with laughter, and we sang for joy. And the other nations said, "What amazing things the Lord has done for them." Yes, the Lord has done amazing things for us! What joy!" Psalms 126:1-3 NLT

Do not let the thoughts, words or actions of imperfect humans affect the **unique being** that you are, created perfectly by and for a **PERFECT** God!

Time to Reflect...

In essence, no one else's words can influence your future unless you accept them. Focus on building your confidence based on your integrity, truthfulness, and excellence. When God created you, He truly made you unique. I dare you to take their words up against God's truth! **God says..." you were created in deep admiration and distinctly separated as you"**!

Stand up in Your Distinction! Reject all voices that contradict this truth! You are wonderful!!

Freedom and peace of mind are your **SUPERPOWER!**

Time to Reflect...

Freedom says I operate in my most authentic self, understanding that all my life experiences make me who I am...good, bad, or indifferent!

Peace says I walk through my day understanding that I have a clean slate within myself and with God!

However, when your environment is inclusive of negativity, we must reflect on the climate.

One of the saddest moments is when a person who claims to love or care about you tries to use your past against you!

Now, it's not sad for you because by blood and the forgiveness of Jesus Christ, you are completely free from condemnation and shame!

It is sad for them...their minds are stuck in a place where God has forgotten and forgiven! They are wasting their mental focus, strategies, and their emotional capital in a space in time that will never return!

Hoping to disrupt your freedom, peace, and growth that they covet!!

Remember, **You are FREE! You are at PEACE!!** *They are stuck! Who's in a better position?*

The limitations that we put on ourselves and others are an **INSULT** to God!

In **His glorious power**, we have more than our minds can comprehend or imagine! We have through **GRACE**: creation power, resurrection power, healing power, delivering power, transformational power, forgiving power, uplifting power, power to speak life into dead situations, and power to recognize that our God can do the impossible with His creation!!

Time to Reflect...

Take the time to ask God for forgiveness for insulting the greatness that He put into you!! Now, reconnect to His grace to meet your needs and move towards your victory!

"Now all glory to God, who is able, through his mighty power at work within us, to accomplish infinitely more than we might ask or think. Glory to him in the church and in Christ Jesus through all generations forever and ever! Amen.". Ephesians 3:20-21 NLT

Grow through what you **go through**! We must all know and concede that we are ever evolving as humans...if you are willing to grow! Sometimes there is fear...and fear can immobilize us. However, we must learn the difference between **healthy fear** and <u>debilitating fear</u>! **Healthy fear** warns us to stop and choose another path, but we do not remain stagnant. Contrary, debilitating fear...keeps us in a hostage position where there is no imaginable escape...thus keeping us in a loop of repeated circumstances of disappointment, hurt, or lack of growth!

Time to Reflect...

Our challenge today is to keep on going and to keep on growing! Live in a transformative mindset, trust in God and yourself to bring you through it all!

But when I am afraid, I will put my trust in you. I praise God for what he has promised. I trust in God, so why should I be afraid?

What can mere mortals do to me?" Psalms 56:3-4,   NLT

Let us focus on the exercise of **ushering peace** into our lives...work, home and in all facets of our being (body, mind, heart, soul and spirit) by learning the practice of **catching the harmful thoughts** and **reframing them to helpful thoughts.**

Time to Reflect...
Remember this truth, your thoughts are under your control and you can shape them to produce PEACE! For every harmful thought, I dare you to find a helpful thought!

There is a quote in the Bible that says, "Do all you can to live at peace with others." If peace is not in you, strive to restore the places in your heart to peace! It is a better life experience when you have peace in your heart, mind and soul.

God, I will trust You, **Heavenly Father!** Thank you for your majestic presence and power. Lord, I'm grateful and appreciative of your love in my life, and the life of my loved ones. I am celebrating your **PRESENCE!!** Why?
Because there is power in your **PRESENCE,**
There is healing in your **PRESENCE**!
There is no fear of conquering our human weakness in your **PRESENCE**!
There is love in your **PRESENCE**!
There is peace in your **PRESENCE**!
There is joy in your **PRESENCE**!

Thank you, Father! No one can steal from you what God provides in His **PRESENCE**!
Hallelujah!
Amen

Time to Reflect...
Take time to consider submitting this as your daily prayer.

Embrace...What should you embrace? **God's love** because no matter where your life has taken you...**His love can meet you there.**

Time to Reflect...

To "embrace" means to take something into your possession or clasp it. I hope you can open your heart and take into your possession the love that God is holding specifically for you. He knows exactly what your heart needs and desires to pour his love into your life...God is love.

You are **NOT** the **SAME!** God commands you to see yourself as **You Have BECOME** in **HIM** and through **HIM** by a relationship with **Christ.**

Time to Reflect...

Upon faith in Christ Jesus, the Savior, believers are positioned in Him and enveloped by His grace.

The gift of salvation grants access to a new life through the Spirit of God, which comes from God through the sacrifice of Jesus Christ, thereby separating us from our former state of sin inherent in our human nature.

The human life is transformed by the spiritual life and God commands us to recognize ourselves as having become a new creation by faith, which provides freedom from darkness, sin, and damnation. It also liberates us from our original self-perception, empowering us to honor God and live by faith. Accept and walk confidently in this newfound identity.

Consider the concept of a **perfect refuge**. Typically, people seek shelter out of fear or look to find rest from difficult situations. However, this idea of refuge implies the absence of fear—no fear of death in life situations, no guilt from choices made, no shame or self-punishment. This concept allows individuals to **experience a sense of protection, mercy, and compassion**.

Time to Reflect...
What are you seeking in your place of perfect refuge?

"You are my hiding place; you will save me from trouble. I sing aloud of your salvation, because you protect me."
Psalm 32:7 GNT

Trusting in God's assurance is an **elevated sense of being!** His **Help** comes because of His love and His faithfulness to Himself and to His word! If His protective **Grace** accompanies you in your daily movements, there is no place you can go without His **accompaniment, authority, and abiding Spirit** in your life.

Time to Reflect...

When you feel like God is not with you, think about the story of the boy in the bubble. He was surrounded by a bubble to protect him from the elements that could hurt him, and this became the normative for his life. Each of us have the awesome privilege to live in the bubble of God's grace, you may not sense it, but it is there!! Furthermore, your bubble is backed up and protected by God's unfailing mercy.

He will protect you as you come and go now and forever."
Psalm 121:8 GNT

If your back is against the wall and you are at a low point in your life, remember this...in God's hands there **beauty** from ashes.
There is **love** from brokenness.
There is **restoration** from impoverishment.
There is **joy** from sadness.
There is **hope** from despair.
There is **peace** from chaos.
There is **clarity** from confusion.
There is **freedom** from bondage
There is...**exactly what you need** because you can encounter the Great I Am!

Time to Reflect...

Find your secret place to meet God, and it there you can receive what He has in store for you.

Whatever you have endured, when **God brings your life into a new state** of being there some **simple facts.**
What you have been through-is over!
What occurred -is no longer happening!
Ways in which lived previously-is not your life!
Words you spoke about yourself-is not your language!
Waffling about getting better- is not where you are in your healing!

Time to Reflect...

Each day as you live by faith, you are changing the internal and external manifestation of yourself that needs to be terminated in order that you can live in a renewal state.
Unearth the destructive cognitions to cancel them and release those thoughts from being your captor.
Cancel the thoughts and emotions one by one and the way you showed up in life that does not create renovation in your spirit, heart, mind, or behavior.
Understand how trauma is rooted in lies, and begin creating a new story of truth about who

you are and how you can react to the lies differently.
Continue to make peace with your journey of healing, knowing that you are living in a new state of the spirit, as God dwells in you.

"Since you have heard about Jesus and have learned the truth that comes from him, throw off your old sinful nature and your former way of life, which is corrupted by lust and deception. Instead, let the Spirit renew your thoughts and attitudes. Put on your new nature, created to be like God—truly righteous and holy."
Ephesians 4:21-24 NLT

A true love affair understands that to operate in its fullness, the love relies on the bedrock of a continual experiential enlightenment of **God's love for you**. This "knowing" enables you to start living as a person loved by God, and allow His love to captivate your body, your heart, soul and spirit to love those who intersect into your life.

Time to Reflect...

Are you searching for true love? Do you feel that something is amiss? Have you taken the time to open the door for God's love to cultivate you and your life? It will be worth your investment in Him and His love!

Empowering You: Body, Mind, Heart, Soul, and Spirit!

Empowering you is the integration of your whole self. Your body, mind, heart, soul and spirit are interconnected, and this requires you to be intentional to inspire and attend to yourself fully.

As you go into this week, seek to recognize that a mistake is not **FINAL**, an error can be corrected, and a disappointment is a lesson for forward movement! **NEVER DIMINISH** yourself due to the lessons you were supposed to **learn!**

Time to Reflect...

When one carries a perfectionist mindset, a mistake can equate to catastrophic thinking, but what would your day be like if you told yourself, "My mistake is my advancement to my next level!" This shift in perspective can alter how one approaches errors.

Take 30-60 seconds to take some deep breaths (breath in, count .3.2.1 and release your breath, repeat) and affirm yourself with this truth!

There are days when you don't feel like doing anything (i.e., work, parenting, engaging with the world), but you push through anyway. **Why do you keep going?** *You are resilient, and life has already TESTED you!*

Time to Reflect...

Resiliency is the bedrock of every new situation that stands before you. Draw from your history to discover what you can do!

Create a resiliency life map to memorialize and remind you of your success.
Include:
What are you learning about your strengths in these moments?
What are you learning about taking the proper rest from your body's cues?
Recognize the body sensations as you uncover your resiliency moments and connect your thoughts/feelings to this experience.
Distinguish if rest or action is needed ~ Resting does foster resilience. Action fosters healthy practice towards coping effectively, but avoidance fosters eventual shutdown as a means of coping with life.

In every space we live and breathe, the ability to move in freedom is a **liberation** for the soul.

Time to Reflect...

If one knows themselves, likes themselves, loves themselves, and lives in their truth; this becomes their navigation through life. What will constitute your liberation? Are you yearning to be free?

Shout Out to each of you because we are all recovering from something in life! No one knows what it takes for each person to **show up** each day!

Time to Reflect...

Shouting You Out because I know you wanted to cry today, but the kids were watching!
Shouting You Out because I know you are feeling pressure to make your finances work!
Shouting You Out because I know you may feel misunderstood in life!
Shouting You Out because you decided to take care of yourself today!
Shouting You Out because your story is someone's inspiration!

What is the "Shout Out" that your spirit is yearning to hear from you? Can you give yourself a "Shout Out?"

Just in case you are feeling overwhelmed or discouraged today, my desire is that you **remain hopeful, as this too shall pass!**

Time to Reflect...

You have overcome so much in your life; you can make it through this very moment! Hold fast to your faith and hope; these two elements are meant to carry you through.

Take time to address your autonomic nervous system responses to achieve grounding. Scan the room from right to left and then left to right, then take deep breaths for 30-60 seconds. Finally, encourage yourself!

In life, we may often feel or perceive ourselves to be stuck in a situation. The reality is that whatever space in your life that feels like a dead end, you have a choice to give yourself permission to operate in courage to turn around and **SEE** the possibilities **AHEAD** of you!

Time to Reflect...

There is always an option and a choice. What possibilities lie ahead for you? Take time to consider what else you can do to help yourself in this situation. Remember, each day that you have a chance and a choice.

Finding **SPIRITUAL REST** for your soul means that God quiets the voices that seek to unsettle your spirit, and you actively receive His word of grace, mercy and peace with certainty! Finding rest in your body means your nervous system relaxes and your rescue mechanism reduces its activation of anxiety. Spiritual rest is rooted in having belief in God to keep his word and promises to you.

Time to Reflect...

Who can recognize your rest better than you? You are the central figure in your life, and your life requires you to show up for you <u>first</u>, so breathe! Exhale to God! Receive His blessings right now! Say thank you, then you can show up for your rest! Go ahead, get started!

If you can, seek not to let your mistakes or failures stop you from staying in the game of life! The mere fact that you got up today speaks to your **ABILITY to step up to the plate**...and if you do not hit a home run today, there is an opportunity to **hit one tomorrow**!

Time to Reflect...

Keep swinging because you will eventually hit the ball. What areas of your life do you need to start swinging the bat to make connections with the difficulties in your life? Journal about this.

Demand that you, your environment, and the universe align with your vision...**SPEAK** what you want in your life and **PURSUE** what you need in your life!

Time to Reflect...

Your language about your life makes a difference! What are you afraid of...there is nothing outside of your reach if it is in the divine order of your life!

In life and relationships, you may find yourself reacting defensively or explaining yourself in response to a comment or an experience. When this occurs, recognize that you owe the world **NO EXPLANATION!**

Time to Reflect...
Tips to address your defensiveness...
1. *Recognize your root thought..., "Am I feeling less than?"; "Do I think others must give me what I want?" or "Am I feeling helpless or treated unfairly?"*
2. *Do I have a choice in accepting this root thought?*
3. *Is there a sense of tension? Could the tension be because I am accepting the internal belief that I owe others an explanation for the choices I make in my life?*
4. *Become aware of your body's signals or reactions and accept what your body is saying to you*
5. *Forgive yourself if you are reacting to a feeling of helplessness or to perfectionism.*
6. *Decide to cultivate self-compassion for yourself and work on changing your*

internal narrative to "I am acceptable!" "Even though I do not get what I want, I am okay." "I have a choice in how I use my energy."." I do not have to defend to cope with this experience, I am okay."
7. Decide to choose your reactions based on the positive internal truth and seek to train your mind to accept a new narrative.
8. Remember, "Everything is not about you! & "Everyone is not against you!"

In life, we can either smell the roses or focus on the thorns, but both aspects of the rose— its beauty and its painful thorns —make the rose complete. Let's choose **gratitude** and **acceptance** for the **beautiful and thorny experiences in life!**

Time to Reflect...

How can you begin this day by embracing radical acceptance that the beauty and thorns of your life were not meant to destroy you, but to reveal who you are... DURABLE, VULNERABLE, POWERFUL and COURAGEOUS!

The **synergy of possessing a growth mindset** says...

"I will fight diligently and collaboratively within myself to come out of a dark place, when I recognize that I am still operating as if I am stuck in the same place."

Time to Reflect...

The growth process suggests that we progress through various stages over time. However, scientific evidence shows that we can physically develop from childhood to adolescence and to adulthood, but internal maturity may advance more gradually. Research has shown if we have a growth mindset that we can support our mental and emotional wellness in favorable ways. It is essential to consciously embrace transitions by abandoning detrimental thought patterns and behaviors. Additionally, we can take the necessary steps to clear our energy and cleanse our soul of any limiting beliefs formed during times of distress, duress, depression, or survival by allowing yourself to grieve, release and growth.

Do not hold on to the right to be angry; it only robs you of **LIVING with JOY and PEACE** in your life.

Time to Reflect...

Chronic sadness may lead to feelings of internal anger, which may impact your ability to live life fully. If you can recognize your sadness as a choice, it could allow you the opportunity to break the agreement with anger. This agreement is a defence mechanism that you think helps you but only harms your growth!

One step at a time, start choosing to take care of you...it could look like...learning how to nurture yourself, address your sadness, exercise, massages, talk therapy, cultivating a small community of support (support groups, etc.) and most importantly faith and hope that this day will be different from yesterday! I speak to you from what I know!

CHOICES, Perspectives and REALITY!

Time to Reflect...

As you rise this morning, consider that your **CHOICES** based on your thoughts could make or break your day. You could choose gratitude or disgruntlement. Depending on your **CHOICES**, it can shape your **PERSPECTIVES** about your day, thus fostering your mind and energy to promote that **REALITY**.

It's within your power to decide to be good and kind to your spirit, then make a **CHOICE** to focus on what you are grateful for; allow this reflection to shape your **PERSPECTIVES** about your life (work, family, relationships); and move into a **REALITY** for your day based on the power of your mind, the energy of your spirit and actions of your body (words and behavior)! Be inspired by gratefulness today!!

HEALING TIME ~ If you need time to heal, no one should be offended by your time clock!

Time to Reflect...

Healing is an essential aspect of our journey at various stages in life. Everyone's healing process is unique and personal. It is important not to feel pressured to expedite the healing process; instead, take the necessary time to address and release the aspects of life that have been holding you back. Subsequently, focus on being present at every moment and prioritizing your peace, progress, and perseverance. Spend time understanding how your body and mind respond to your triggers, this is typically your default survival response. Start to build in practices that allow you to regulate your space for experiencing personal safety. Your healing is nestled inside of your development of personal safety.

Having an **abundance mindset** means you acknowledge that you are human while holding **optimism** in your thoughts and distributing grace to your being. You maintain a set of encouraging attitudes toward yourself and others, which enables you to manage your life's perceptions in ways that can be beneficial rather than harmful.

Time to Reflect...

Living in the present is one way to cultivate an abundant mindset. Work to stay present, positive and have continual daily practices to ground your nervous system states (hyperarousal or hypo-arousal) towards a sense of safety. When you sense safety, it creates opportunity for powerful viewpoints about yourself and life.

Living with the **principle of good intent** means we assume good intentions (unless the empirical evidence counters that notion), but **we take responsibility** to ask a clarifying question, for example, "Can you share what you meant by that...?" Accept the response if it indicates the other person did not want to cause harm to you.

Time to Reflect...

How often have you had disagreements due to not following the principle of good intent? In what ways could you foster the principle of good intent into your life and relationships?

Stop underestimating your power to get through the hard moments in your life! Think of how **God had your back** and the **fortitude you have established for the next adverse situation that may happen in your life.** It's about understanding your resolve. Resolve is your ability to remain steadfast and focused on the end goal. Recognize how much tenacity you already have at your access!

Time to Reflect...

Draw upon your determination and resolve, then reflect on your memories of the times when you made it through a difficult time.

.

Emotional maturity is not about age or experience; it is about one's ability to be **self-aware of one's emotional integrity.** Additionally, it is about refusing to compromise one's emotional integrity with someone who lacks emotional intelligence.

Time to Reflect...

Steady yourself, focus your energy and find your truth to guide you to a place of emotional integrity, no matter what comes your way today! This level of integrity can produce greater insight and clarity about who you are and becomes a means to your personal growth.

If you find that your thoughts often dwell on what you lack, take some time to reflect on your surroundings, contemplate your relationships with friends and family, assess your overall health, and evaluate your available resources, even if they are limited. Then, **allow** yourself to **appreciate the abundance that is present in your life**.

Time to Reflect...

Your abundant mindset can emerge when you realize, even in your worst circumstances, that there is something you have that someone else may desire. Seek an abundant mindset, and you will find it!

If you have the consideration to appreciate someone else's contribution or attributes, then pause and **LOOK** in the mirror and *appreciate* your own contributions and attributes! Your efforts are justifiably **FANTASTIC** as well!

Time to Reflect...

You can be your #1 fan and remain humble. Do not let fear stop you from being uniquely you. List at least two affirming thoughts that value your unique qualities.

Rainbows are said to offer us a sign of **HOPE** or be the **BEAUTY** after the storm...so as we move through our day, we do not know if our **ACT OF KINDNESS** can equal a **RAINBOW** to someone's stormy day.

Time to Reflect...

Imagine how blessed you will feel knowing your kindness was the gift that the other person needed. How can you let your kindness shine to yourself and others today?

Embracing Love & Compassion for Yourself!

Embracing love and compassion for yourself is about your love tank. When we have a full love tank for ourselves, our ability to have abundant love becomes more prevalent. Our ability to hug ourselves is the basis of self-compassion and emotional regulation, fostering the space to care and nurture ourselves.

Learning to love yourself is one of the initial steps to having **meaningful relationships.** If you can love yourself unconditionally, you can offer love to others with empathy and compassion...it starts with you **FIRST~**

Time to Reflect...

Love is free! Love is spiritual! Love is unconditional! Love is concerned for the well-being of others and yourself! Love must be nurtured! Ultimately, love comes from God, but the question becomes, "Will you dare to accept love?"

What does 'Daring to Accept Love' look like?

Daring to Accept Love means being grateful for a beating heart, an active mind, and physical health.
Daring to Accept Love means being willing to ask for help.
Daring to Accept Love means being able to acknowledge your personal needs.
Daring to Accept Love means...being okay with accepting someone's support in your life!
Daring to Accept Love means...operating in a cyclical love affair with life, not a one-sided love

(you give and never receive or you take and never give)!

Daring to Accept Love *means seeing the blessings that life provides, even if these blessings seem small.*

Daring to Accept Love *means...forgiving yourself for your humanity and forgiving others for their humanity!*

Finally, **Daring to Accept Love** *will initiate the healing that your heart seeks and give you the capacity to self-care!*

Give yourself a second chance to **Dare to Accept Love** *Today!*

For **healing,** it is essential to have two components of love ~ One is being able to receive the love **that is all around you** and Two, is being able to receive love **from you for yourself.** Embrace the love **that awaits** you!

Time to Reflect...

Close your eyes right now! Now, imagine how different you will look, feel and think if you could embrace the love that is surrounding and waiting for you to notice its presence! Can you see it? Who are you? Look at your power!!

The person that **you are**...is good enough no matter what has been said about you, and no matter what you say to yourself! **Embrace yourself** and what you bring to the table!

Time to Reflect...
Inhaling your uniqueness is a joy to God, since He created you. You must know and believe that what He did in your creation was GOOD!

YOU ARE PUMPING UP YOUR RESOLVE BECAUSE...Freedom requires not only for you to come out of untenable situations, but to break the chains of a bondage mindset and cleanse the soul!

Time to Reflect...

What is necessary in your life to move into freedom? Reflect on the value of your freedom. What does it mean to you? Freedom moves beyond a change in thinking, and it entails that the patterns created in your body (desires, repetitive responses to distress or willpower) find another pathway to operate in that releases you from harming yourself to helping yourself.

My hope is that each person can **SEE**, **EXPERIENCE**, and **KNOW** the **LOVE** that radiates in your life, despite any circumstances...always look for **LOVE** first!

Time to Reflect...

One has asked this question, "Why do I deserve this generosity to see love in my life?" The answer is because God has shined the light on the love that is inside of you that needs to be fulfilled in this space of your life. There are love representatives available to you...if you can open your eyes to these gifts!

Enjoy the skin that you are in because there is **NOT A Replacement** for YOU!

Time to Reflect...

What would the world be without your presence? We need you in this world because you are irreplaceable. Think about it!

Remember, **YOU** are the **mission**!! Many times, we may spend our efforts trying to help someone else, support a cause, assist a loved one, or support a group. Often, we find ourselves depleted without hope, depressed, sad or feeling empty. It is because we forgot along the way that helping others, that you too, are the **mission!**

Don't forget to care for and love yourself!

Time to Reflect...

You matter too! Find ways to pursue different types of rest to support your recovery from giving to others. Try physical rest when your body calls for sleep or relaxation. Try emotional rest by honoring your boundaries or self-acceptance. Try mental rest when your mind is focused on helping others such as taking breaks or scheduling time to worry. Try sensory rest when over-stimulated by turning off your phone or sitting still quietly. Try co-regulation by social interaction within safe spaces. Try praying or meditation when spirit needs nourishing. Try to cross your arms, grab your outer elbows, and hug yourself today! You need a hug, too!

Self-love must encompass treating your human vessel as a **receptacle of love**. Before we can accept love from others, it is essential to cultivate genuine **self-love**. This involves not superficial admiration, but the kind of unconditional love that we aspire to receive from significant individuals in our lives, though it is often lacking.

Time to Reflect...

Let your human vessel embrace love that says:
I am okay with all my frailties.
I am okay despite my past.
I am enough.
I am a work in progress.
I am casting off my fears.
I am beautiful internally and externally as God created me!

VALUE LIVING looks like making this daily commitment to yourself. "I will allow myself permission to **REDISCOVER** and **RECOGNIZE** the value of my authentic voice! I will choose to live a lifestyle that honors my person!

Time to Reflect...

Look up the definitions of the words value and honor, then write your own personal affirmation based on the definitions to live by.

In life, there may be family or fair-weather friends who may not have supported you or loved you for the beautiful human that God created, so **IT IS TIME** for **YOU** to start **LOVING YOURSELF!**

Time to Reflect...

Today, give yourself the gift of commencing your self-love journey. You can start with one simple step, by looking in the mirror for at least 3-4 minutes each day and speak those three words..." I LOVE YOU" ...to yourself!

Walk in the **MIRACLE** of **PEACE** in your life as you choose to **ACCEPT** yourself and **ACCEPT** that you are powerless over others, but you are **POWERFUL** over **YOU!**

Time to Reflect...

As you meditate on your power of choice, seek to give yourself permission to do something helpful for you. How can you reclaim your power of choice for this day?

You cannot say that you have **hope** and only speak negatively or with gloom and doom.

Time to Reflect...

Remember that self-love requires you to pay attention to your language (internally and externally. What you say to yourself can usher in positive experiences or negative experiences. Which do you desire? Practice the following actions to shift your negative thinking to positive thinking:

- *Take the time to become aware of the words that you speak!*
- ***Take into consideration using language that fosters growth, healing, and empowerment.***
- *Target your choices to reclaim your voice to bring change in your life!*

Remember, **YOU** are as **GREAT** as **YOU** can **SEE** yourself **BEING!**

Time to Reflect...

Greatness is not a theory...it is a pursuit. No...it is not about your monetary value! It is the greatness in your character, your integrity, your consistency in your words, your compassion and empathy, your authenticity, and you fulfilling your purpose! Maybe today you cannot see your greatness, so my charge to you is to start cleaning off your internal lenses to believe in yourself and watch your greatness start to emerge in your life.

Believe in what you **see** and **experience!**

Believe in your **inner voice** that speaks from **LIGHT** versus darkness!

Believe in your **STRENGTH** in your weakest moments of **LIFE!**

Time to Reflect...

If your life has been difficult, and you wondered if you were going to make it. Let me tell you a little secret, look at the historical evidence. You are buoyant, and those experiences did not break you. Start a historical review of the many times you have made it against odds...that is your superpower!

I will not deny my feelings for anyone. I will honor and value my voice and where I'm at in my life. I know what is **healthy** for me.

Time to Reflect...

The art of personal authenticity means that I learn the practice of identifying and experiencing emotional maturation with my daily feelings. When you reconnect to your emotions, you will find that your emotions can be less intimidating and nothing for you to fear.

Today, you have found your words and your words may sting, but **you will not be silent!**
Today, you have fortified your soul from years of pain., and **you will not be silent!**
Today, you have gained true wisdom by watching and listening to what others do verses what they say, so **you will not be silent!**
Today, you have a plethora of truth to reveal, and **you will not be silent!**
Today, you have finally broken the proverbial muzzle from the years of shame, so, **you will not be silent!**
Today, you can choose to let your heart soar from the authenticity of who **YOU** are... you **CANNOT be SILENT**!

Time to Reflect...

I will not be silent as I am purposed to live in truth, reveal the truth, encourage other souls to be free and loved in the beauty of which God created them to be. SILENCE is not an option!

Steady Love is a component of our self-love and compassion. The distinction is to maintain steady and consistent love as life takes us on the multitude of experiences.

Time to Reflect...

Your self-love can be defined as forgiveness, freedom and fortification of your heart! As your soul searches for external confirmation of care and concern, settle the soul with the imparted truth in your mind and spirit with these simple words, "I love you!" I love my creation!" "I love my life"!

Instead of seeing the areas of growth as negative aspects of yourself, seek to see these areas as opportunities to **excel beyond your wildest imagination**!

Time to Reflect...

Commence the process of releasing the limiting negative self-talk to being kind to yourself with a love affair with your mind, body and soul!

Do something for your good today

A fundamental gift to this life is to **learn who you are**. Why is this discovery a mandate for living? When you know yourself, no one can move you or push you beyond your boundaries. You choose your direction because in your **true self**, your ability to weigh the options originates from knowing what is best for you and you **KNOW YOU!**

Time to Reflect...

Self-discovery is never an antiquated practice for your personal growth and evolution. If you are questioning who you are today, seek to start the acquisition of the gift of self-discovery.

Self-love breeds HOPE! **Hope** that can fill the empty spaces! **Hope** that revives self-motivation! **Hope** that garners fuel for the journey of life! **Hope** that can heal the wounded places of your heart! **Hope** that can give you permission to give yourself a second chance!

Time to Reflect...

Inventory your self-love meter, and if it is low, make efforts to fill it with grace, compassion, acceptance, patience, gentleness, faith, joy and self-control. Reclaim your love and reclaim your hope.

Purposeful Living!

The art of purposeful living commences with understanding the genesis of your life, grasping the truth that your life matters and giving everything you have within yourself to make a life impact!

Do not just do LIFE but **LIVE your LIFE!** Your living can be a manifestation of your history, your healing, your hope and your **HYPE!**

Time to Reflect...

One day you may wake up to the realization that life has taken over you and somewhere on the journey you forgot to LIVE. However, your life has purpose and you do not have to fear living with your excellence. Your life cannot be stifled by the words of others, so RISE up as the person who carries the backbone of generational strength and courage. RISE to answer the clarion call to live out your vision with passion and confidence!

Live your life by being **present** in each moment and experience the essence of those moments through sight, smell, hearing, taste and touch. Pay attention to the gift of what your sensory offers your life. Do not let robotic living rob you of your **precious moments**.

Time to Reflect...

What moment are you experiencing now? What could be blocking you from being present? Which one of your senses brings you awareness in being uniquely you! Do not let your feelings unchecked by your empirical logic run rampant as you live each day!

You cannot be **COMPARED** to your old self. You cannot be **COMPARED** to yourself yesterday...Why? You have changed! As the earth rotates around the sun every day, there is no possibility for you to be in the same space and time. As each new day offers new chances, new mercies and new opportunities to do something different than you did the day before!

Time to Reflect...
Let no one convince you that you are not growing. Believe in the evolution of yourself. What will you do differently today to support your forward movement and stop comparing your today to your yesterday?

Let your **success** be measured this week by all those things that you do that no one notices...**Salute Yourself**!

Time to Reflect...

You deserve to take credit for what you bring to the table and what you do! Celebrate everything that you try! The effort that you put forth in the attempts is worth celebrating! Celebrate the small wins!

Just because they agree with you, does not mean they are on **your team**!

Time to Reflect...

All agreements are not for you or good for you. Remember, Satan disguise himself as an angel of light. This means it may look good, soothe you, and sound good to what you want, but it may be meant for your destruction. Pay attention to the history of the individual. Pray for the words of advice coming to you. Ponder the motivations of the guidance you received and your own motivations. Position yourself to hear from God. He is the ultimate Person on your team!

The beauty of our lives is that we get an opportunity every day to create a life impact! Let the **GENESIS** of your impact start **WITHIN**, then it will **RIPPLE** out to all that you intersect with each day!

Time to Reflect...

You decide…who will be impacted today because you choose to take care of yourself today!

Our **purpose** and **passion** for life are driven by what is in our hearts. Never neglect your inward compass to fulfill that *"thing"* that is most important to you and that will create a legacy!

Time to Reflect...

Be intentional and meticulous about what your imprint will be on this world. Write down your vision for your legacy, outline the next steps you will take to fulfill your vision. Each day, chose to take steps towards your purpose, even if it is a half-a step...remember it is a step!

Take each **opportunity** to be **present** to experience each moment to the fullest and continue to evolve as you become more authentically **YOU** each day!

Time to Reflect...

Are you living robotically, or are you embracing each moment? Imagine what you are missing because you are too worried about the future or too sad about the past.

There is NO stronger voice than the one inside of you that tells you that, "**You got this!**", "**You will be okay!**" "**You are stronger than you know!**" "**You were made for this instant in time!**" Say it through tears and through your fears until you believe it!

Time to Reflect...

Work to let your inner advocate outweigh the fears and cheer yourself all the way to victory! If you struggle to find or hear your inner advocate, think about what you would say to a friend or a family member who needed your support. Let that same advocacy statements become your inner voice. If you gave them to someone else, you have them in you…to offer to yourself.

No better time than the present...to show up as **YOU!!** Never let others' perceptions, comments, or ideas of you manifest into your destiny!

Time to Reflect...

Whose life are you choosing to live if you are not showing up each day as you? Reflect on the ways that you may alter yourself to please others or avoid being yourself to make others comfortable. Now, ask yourself, "Is this serving you?"

What are you afraid of? Start to show up as "authentically you" EVERY SECOND OF THE DAY!

Learning to **heal** is one of the initial steps to having meaningful relationships. If you can **allow healing into your mind, body, spirit, heart and soul**, you can offer a healthiness that is refreshing to your soul and impactful to the people within your sphere of life.

Time to Reflect...

When we have unmet needs or emotional healing needed because of not being nurtured in childhood or hold psychological wounds, we often seek out people or fives to fill the gaps! Most often these attractions are not good for us.

Healing yourself first allows us to fill the gaps in healthy ways, then your relationships will mirror and emote healthy boundaries, love freedom and mutual respect.

Each day, life offers you **a new lesson** about yourself. There is something **remarkable** about these opportunities because they are filled with ***possibilities*** of growth, accomplishment and fulfillment.

Time to Reflect...

Figuring out who you are is the best gift you can give to yourself, your friends, family and children. Life is your schoolbook! Life offers a new lesson to you daily and to those in your circle and those yet to come into your life. Do not take for granted that you do not have more lessons to learn. Embrace it and walk in courage!

STOP working overtime to be **UNDERSTOOD** and **VALUED**!

Time to Reflect...

Here is the question for self-reflection. Why am I pressing so hard for someone else to get my authenticity?

Some individuals may find it challenging to look beyond their own experiences and perspectives. It is essential to recognize this limitation, accept reality, and redirect your efforts towards more productive and constructive areas of your life.

Embrace **VALUED LIVING** as your mantra and gift yourself with this commitment----I will **allow** myself **permission** to rediscover and recognize the **value** of my authentic voice, and I will choose a lifestyle that **honors** my truest self.

Time to Reflect...

Take a moment and reflect on these two words:
Value – meaning to have relative worth, utility and importance.
Honor – meaning to have a keen sense of ethical conduct, integrity, one whose worth brings respect.
Now, I want you to determine where and how you will operate "Valued Living" in your life, to manifest value and honor.

Never underestimate the audacity of God to pursue you to elevation despite your circumstances.

Time to Reflect...

The audacity of God does not care how long you been in your situation. The audacity of God does not care what people have said about you. The audacity of God does not care how long you have been avoiding or denying what He has to offer you. His pursuit will not stop until He has achieved what He designed for your life when you were in crafted in your mother's womb. His plan is definite...EMBRACE HIS AUDACITY FOR YOU!

It is a funny thing that happens when you realize that you were created for **PURPOSE** and **NOT** for **DESTRUCTION!**

You detach from people, energy, and environments, and you commence focusing your thoughts and emotions to align with living your purpose.

Time to Reflect...

What are you going to do today to walk in your purpose? Time is of the essence, and all of us need your purpose to be revealed and actualized, and history to take notice!

Today as you rise...**make the choice to stay in power!** Staying in power is not about aggression or always assertion...it is about owning you, your values and your voice! It is setting boundaries when people seek to break them! It is holding your internal core at peace when life or the winds of chaos approaches and swirls around you! It is knowing when to stand on principle and when compromise is available to you! Staying in power is YOU...100% **Authentically YOU!** You are not perfect but you were divinely crafted to be **Unapologetically YOU!**

Time to Reflect...

Are you confident in who you are? What stands out when you think about being authentically you? Create your elevator pitch, but instead of telling it to someone else, say it to YOU!

Today is your day to **SHINE**!

Time to Reflect...

Shining is all about the outlook that one possesses! The sun will appear after a storm, and this is the hope that you can carry within...this day can be better than yesterday. Have hope and faith, reach for the light in your life and allow it to shine through you!

Remember, there can be **goodness** in you, but let your **goodness be driven by godliness** as you determine what matters to you!

Time to Reflect...

Goodness is typically measured by a human assessment, so there is potential for us all to possess goodness. However, someone can always profess that your goodness does not measure their measurement of what is good. But no one can remove your goodness that is driven by godliness because the source is Divine, and it originates from God. So, let this truth remain, "I seek godliness that proves my goodness to myself, this is what matters to me."

The past could hold you hostage if you let it! However, it only takes **ONE SECOND** to take your **AUTHORITY** and **WALK** in the **LIGHT** of your **PURPOSEFULNESS** and your **FUTURE!**

Time to Reflect...

Encouraging you to tap into your authority to shift this very moment to reclaim one thing that brings light, joy, inner peace, balance, or mindfulness into your daily life. You will not regret it!

Transcending Higher!

As we approach life, we may have some limiting beliefs, but transcending higher in our lives creates a unique opportunity for us to believe higher, think higher, operate in a higher state of being, to move us from stagnant spaces to elevated experiences in life.

If you want a different existence in your life, stop making excuses and **EXECUTE** the very thing that you claim you want! You owe no one your aspirations but **YOURSELF**.

Time to Reflect...

Don't talk about it: Be about it!
Execution is in your DNA. How many times have you faced a problem and you analyzed the issue, created a solution and executed to solve the problem. Stop waiting to exercise your ability to execute your transformation!
It is in you!
Don't talk about it: Be about it!

Seek to take on the practice of **NOT COMPARING** yourself to yesterday. There is no opportunity in seeking to relive a day that no longer exists. We can only learn from yesterday. Remember, you will not be the same today as you were yesterday...Why...today is a **NEW** day!

Time to Reflect...

Can you take on this affirmation? I will no longer live as the person that I was yesterday, but I be the person this NEW day brings me.
~Learn from it
~Grow from it
~It's New Day

Some of our **most significant** life lessons are because we dared to try, and our attempts came up short. We learned from our **FAILURES** and our **RESOLVE** to pursue the things that matter most to us!

Time to Reflect...

How can you use your failures and resolve to push yourself through this moment?

Just in case you are having a bad moment in your day, it does not mean your entire day must be defined as "bad". You only need the operation of a deliberate mental **ADJUSTMENT** to turn the channel of your mental scenery from the catastrophe towards an alternate movie that **ALLOWS** you options to come out as a winner! The direction of your day is up to you... shift to something different!

Time to Reflect...

Learning the practice of interrupting the negative images in your mind will give you peace. Your thoughts are subject to your control. Remember this!

Being courageous is not the absence of fear, but it means **TAKING A RISK** on yourself to move to your next level!

Time to Reflect...

Celebrating your courage today. Keep going, "Risk Taker!"

Sometimes the road you are walking on becomes crowded with barriers or has too many detours; in those cases, you are not obligated to stay on that road. Use the **POWER** of your **PREROGATIVE** and your **INGENUITY** to create another path forward!

Time to Reflect...

Never let the barriers stop you from pursuing your path. What changes are needed to clear the road?

The lens of **HOPE**! This view guides us NOT to look at life through the lens of fear --- with what you cannot have, BUT to look at life through the lens of possibilities and opportunities of what you can have!

Time to Reflect...

In times of despair and hopelessness, it can be difficult to see the light of hope. In these moments, seek to find at least three things that you are grateful for in your life. Focus on things such as…the air you are breathing, the smell of your home, the touch of a soft blanket, the picture of you in happier times, the sounds of your favorite melody and the taste of your favorite food! The mere fact that you have all five senses and breath…is a reason to say, "Thank you!"

Living is a small word that holds so much promise and power! Why?
Many of us have not found the formula to "**LIVING**", we only operate in the context of our lives robotically versus experiencing the **BEAUTY** of our lives!

Time to Reflect...

Living holds the promise of giving us new experiences, new lessons, and new opportunities to grow, heal and evolve!

Living has the power to teach us to be present with each person or situation we encounter daily.

It is up to us if we choose to live.

So, each day, when you open your eyes, take a deep breath and exhale, scan your room, count all your blessings, send gratitude vibes, and let every moment today be worth it. Give your all to each moment and simply start LIVING.

Think higher of **YOURSELF!** Think higher of **OTHERS** in your life! Think higher for your **DREAMS**! Think higher of what you will **ACCOMPLISH** on this day! Even when life disappoints you and people in your life have caused you some form of hurt, you have the remarkable ability to **CHOOSE** to elevate your thoughts to a higher vibration. Have integrity about your feelings, address how your body is reacting to the experience and allow yourself the gift of **THOUGHT LIBERATION** by going higher in your thinking.

Time to Reflect

What area in your life today needs thought liberation? Thought liberation teaches you that it is not your job to point out every flaw in a person or yourself; it's your job to build, strengthen and honor your mind, body and soul so integrity, love, kindness, peace and self-respect govern the way you see yourself and show up to life.

Do not let your setbacks impede your **COMEBACK**! Our journey in life is filled with unpredictable moments, despite our best-laid plans. When you encounter one of these unpredictable moments, direct your mind to your empirical evidence of days when you conquered your fears, the times you achieved success, and the moments when your determination propelled you forward. You have been here before, and you were able to overcome!

Time to Reflect *It is natural to become anxious or unsettled with something that happens in life that was outside of your plan or vision, but it is how you manage those experiences that allows you to overcome them immediately or delay your recovery time.*

Place your hand on your chest and take a breath...

Focus your inner thoughts on this affirmation, "Yes, I am disappointed, but I am not alone in this experience."

Rally your inner advocate to encourage you on through this moment. Give yourself permission to win.

It is natural to become anxious or unsettled with something that happens in life that was outside of your plan or vision, but it is how you manage those experiences that allows you to overcome them immediately or delay your recovery time.

Place your hand on your chest and take a breath...

Focus your inner thoughts on this affirmation, "Yes, I am disappointed, but I am not alone in this experience."

Rally your inner advocate to encourage you on through this moment. Give yourself permission to win.

If **HISTORY** has educated you in life, **REMEMBER** you do not need the same lesson twice!

Time to Reflect...

One key to living is allowing your past to inform your current decisions. Particularly, if your history lesson was a situation that produced unfavorably outcomes. Time doesn't change this truth; it only solidifies your education, because 10 times out of 10, this was God's safety plan for you. Use the wisdom gained from this lesson and turn off the internal message that says, 'Try again.' The outcome will not change...you will have to change your choices.

Do not be afraid of **NEW HORIZONS!** Each morning, the sun rises across the horizon. Each night, the moon appears on the dust of the night. It is the set order of life... learn to embrace the new opportunities each day brings to you.

Time to Reflect...

One of the most crippling spaces you could find yourself living in is being afraid of letting go. When you let go, it only means that something better is on the horizon for you and your life! Learning to condition the mind to see what CAN BE versus what cannot be is the key!

ACCEPTANCE over **ACCUSATION** is the key!

Time to Reflect... *The first relationship that we want to focus on is the relationship that we have with ourselves! If you are prone to punishing yourself for your choices, you will never be able to move to a place of healing and transformation.*

Learn to practice acceptance over accusation! This can usher in peace and confidence!
Say these words to yourself, "I accept me".
Say these words to yourself, "I accept my uniqueness".
Say these words to yourself, "I accept my feelings and that I will resolve the rational vs the irrational as I have time to process my emotions".
Say these words to yourself, "I accept that I am much more powerful than I imagine"!
Seek to pay attention to what acceptance feels like physically, emotionally, spiritually and mentally, then Walk in acceptance!

The **MEASURE** of your power is connected to your mindset and how each person filters information ~

Your **POWER** says, "if it rains, I will choose to look for the **RAINBOW**"!

Your **POWER** says, "if I am experiencing disappointment, you will choose to keep **HOPE** for better times"!

Your **POWER** says, "if I fail on the 1st, 2nd, and 3rd attempt, I will choose to try and try again"!

Your **POWER** says, "if you hurt me, I will choose to forgive for the betterment of my heart and peace of mind"!

Keeping **MY POWER** says that I believe in **ME**!

Time to Reflect...

How much of your strength are you willing to cultivate? Step out! Step forward! Step into your power at this moment, on this day.

Do not let the negativity of life experiences outweigh your gratefulness. **Gratefulness** is a feeling or demonstration of appreciation of kindness or being appreciative of the benefits received in your life. Take a moment to **OPEN** your **EYES** and see all your **BENEFITS!**

Time to Reflect...

Build the practice of saying "Thank You!" Release the negative tension that belonged to yesterday and choose to intentionally promote good thoughts for today! Choose to see your benefits!

The only way to hold someone **accountable** is to *hold yourself accountable*. Integrity matters to your psyche, your internal dialogue and the patterns in your relationships!

Time to Reflect...

Start to spend more time tracking if you are keeping your word to yourself. If you find that you are lacking self-accountability, create an exercise of rewards for accountability.

The more you can see yourself relying on YOU, it will increase your ability to show yourself that you can trust your instincts.

Living beyond the moment *is a part of living in the moment.* The past is the past...yesterday is the past! A moment ago, it is now the past! There is nothing that can be done with the seconds or moments that have gone by, other than determining to learn from the moment to allow your next moment to be what you want it to be.

Time to Reflect...

What does your moment teach you about your life? Are you ready to move beyond the moment in acceptance, no judgement, forgiveness or hope? Are you ready to live free of regrets? If so, then live like a conqueror that you are!

Never allow anyone to diminish you! Your life context is **meaningful and exceptional!** Your feelings and your thoughts, whether collided with pain or joy, are beautiful because these are **elements of your being!** While evolution may be on the menu, if someone else cannot see you by your shared experience with them or your verbalized expression, then it is their issue to evolve, and your right to stand in you!

Time to Reflect...

Stop wasting your time considering another person's opinion of you. Do not let their words penetrate your heart, soul and mind. Eliminate the voices that seek to diminish your remarkable existence.

There is a distinction between **wanting** to do something and being **willing** to exert all necessary effort to attain it.

If you lack the desire to pursue a goal, you will find reasons to avoid it. Conversely, if you are committed to achieving something, you will identify reasons to act.

Time to Reflect...

What is holding you back from what you tell yourself and others that you want? Take the time to identify your barriers, address them, and choose to be integral towards yourself. Invest in learning how to fortify and honor your mental, emotional, physical and spiritual self to increase your willpower to achieve your goals. Settle into the belief that your goals are worth fighting for. Accept the tension that the decision may bring into your life. Remain steadfast and know that your goals will come to fruition.

You are worth being free! It just takes one courageous step at time.

Time to Reflect

Step into your peace by courageously telling yourself the truth about the areas of your life that need evolution.

Speak your hidden truth to someone who is trustworthy of hearing your vulnerability, remembering not every person deserves your vulnerability.

Separate out the energies from your life that promote your lack of freedom.

Set yourself up for small victories by recognizing that mental and emotional freedom is foreign to you and captivity is always lurking to step back in as your pseudo friend.

See yourself operating differently in freedom by drawing a picture or a vision of you walking freely in a meadow of flowers, creating new narratives in your coping skills.

Strengthen your muscle memory by practicing new coping skills and operate a new way of being and doing life.

Surrender to what is healthy, healing and hopeful for your recovery.

Your **Power of Permission** is your gateway to change! Why? PERMISSION means to "Giving Consent", and TO PERMIT means "To Allow". Radical shifts require you to give yourself consent to do something different and to allow yourself to engage in the process of change verses resisting your transformation.

Time to Reflect...

Give yourself consent for self-love and self-acceptance.
Allow yourself the recognition of your beauty of who you are as a human being existing on this earth!

Give yourself consent to forgive.
Allow the peace of forgiveness to release your patterns characterised by self-criticism, self-defeating actions, and tendencies toward self-sabotage!

Give yourself consent to heal.
Allow the grieving process from the loss that you have experienced in your life and from the expectations in life that have not been fulfilled!

Give yourself consent to let go.
Allow the freedom that emerges when you operate from courage to step forward into a new space in your mind, heart, soul and spirit.

Give yourself consent to have hope.
Allow your mind to create a new vision of your life in forward movement from your past!

Give yourself consent to be content but not complacent.
Allow the emergence of happiness and joy as a daily disposition appreciating the gifts, miracles and blessings in your life!

Give yourself consent to breathe.
Allow the life-giving breath of God to bring wholeness to life!

References

All quotes and words of inspiration are from the author ~ Dr. Lisa Cook

Shershun, E. (2021). *Healing Sexual Traumatic Workbook: Somatic Skills To Help You Feel Safe In Your Body, Create Boundaries & Live with Resilience.* New Harninger Publications, Inc.: Oakland, CA.

Cook, L. (2020) *Coming Out: How to Reclaim Your Power and Live Your Authentic Truth to Create Life Impact!* Life Impact Circles: Illinois

Tao W, Zhao D, Yue H, Horton I, Tian X, Xu Z, Sun HJ. *The Influence of Growth Mindset on the Mental Health and Life Events of College Students.* Front Psychol. 2022 Apr 14;13:821206. doi: 10.3389/fpsyg.2022.821206. PMID: 35496212; PMCID: PMC9046553.